Jonah and the Big Fish

God told Jonah to preach in Nineveh. But Jonah hopped on a boat going to Tarshish instead.

1

Bad weather tossed the boat. The sailors knew Jonah was running from the Lord. "It's my fault," Jonah said.

2

Jonah jumped out of the boat and into the mouth of a big fish that God had sent to save him.

3

Jonah was inside the fish for 3 days and nights. The Lord commanded the fish to cough Jonah onto dry land.

4

God spoke to Jonah again about Nineveh. This time, Jonah obeyed.

5

The people of Nineveh were glad that God sent Jonah to preach to them.

6

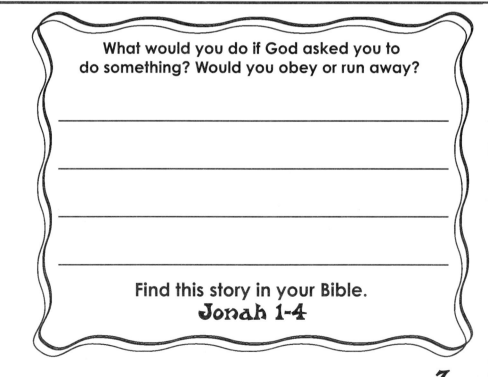

What would you do if God asked you to do something? Would you obey or run away?

_____

_____

_____

_____

Find this story in your Bible.
Jonah 1-4

7

2

After all, Esau was a strong, hairy hunter. Jacob was as smooth as a baby.

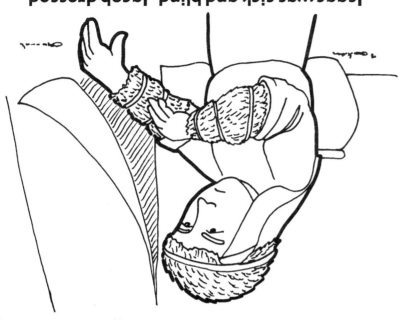

3

Isaac was sick and blind. Jacob dressed in animal hair to trick his father.

Jacob's Deceit

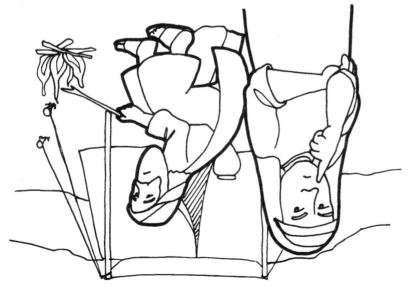

1

Isaac had a blessing for Esau that Jacob wanted. How could Jacob pretend to be Esau to receive the blessing?

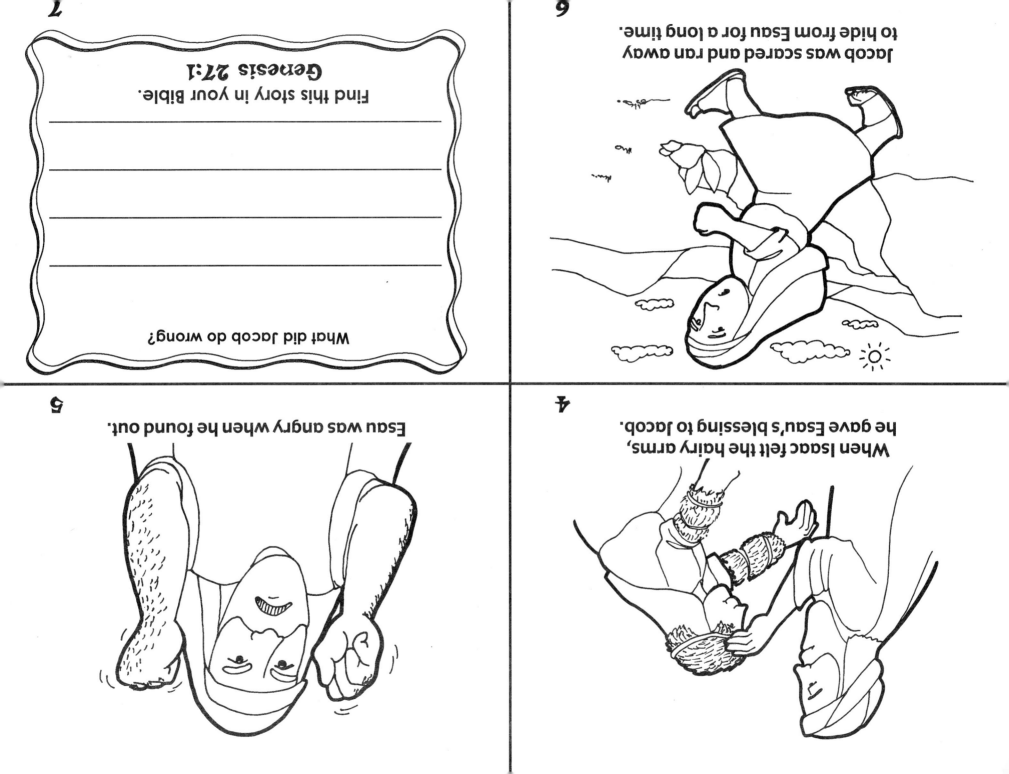

7

What did Jacob do wrong?

Find this story in your Bible.
Genesis 27:1

6

Jacob was scared and ran away
to hide from Esau for a long time.

5

Esau was angry when he found out.

4

When Isaac felt the hairy arms,
he gave Esau's blessing to Jacob.

Old Testament Take-Home Bible Stories

Easy-to-Make, Reproducible Mini-Books
That Children Can Make and Keep

by
Thomas C. Ewald

Illustrations by
Joni Oeltjenbruns

Carson-Dellosa Christian Publishing

© 2003, Carson-Dellosa Publishing Company, Inc., Greensboro, North Carolina 27425. The purchase of this material entitles the buyer to reproduce activities and worksheets for home or classroom use only—not for commercial resale. Reproduction of these materials for an entire school or district is prohibited. No part of this book may be reproduced (except as noted above), stored in a retrieval system, or transmitted in any form or by any means (mechanically, electronically, recording, etc.) without the prior written consent of Carson-Dellosa Publishing Co., Inc.

Printed in the USA • All rights reserved.

ISBN 0-88724-871-3

Credits

Editor: Carol Layton
Layout Design: Mark Conrad
Inside Illustrations: Joni Oeltjenbruns
Cover Design: Annette Hollister–Papp
Cover Illustration: Dan Sharp

Table of Contents

About This Book

Old Testament Take-Home Bible Stories contains 62 stories for children to color and make into their very own story books! The last page of each book contains a question about the story and a Scripture reference to one of the key verses of the story. Use this reference to teach children how to locate passages in their Bibles, and then read the story to them. Reading from the Bible is an excellent way to teach the story and to enrich children's hearts and minds with the beauty and power of the Living Word. Making the take-home book is a fun and interactive way to supplement this Bible reading. (The captions in the take-home books are paraphrases rather than direct quotations from Scripture.) As you discuss the application questions, lead children to understand that the God of the Bible—the God of Moses, David, and Esther—is also their God. He desires to fellowship with them, provide for them, and deliver them just as He has always done for His people. He is the same yesterday, today, and forever!

How to Make the Take-Home Books

You may choose to remove the pages (1a), or make copies directly from the book (1b).

1a. To remove pages: Carefully separate the page along the perforation. To reduce the risk of tearing, first score the perforation with a craft knife or a scissors tip. Align the page with the guides on the copy machine, making sure to place the perforated side away from any edge on the machine. Make single-sided copies of the page on standard 8 1/2" x 11" paper.

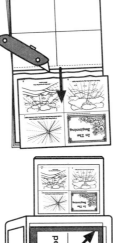

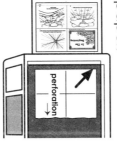

1b. To copy directly from book: Open the book and place it as flat as possible on the copy machine and make single-sided copies on standard 8 1/2" x 11" paper.

2. Trim the edge close to where the perforation was (if following 1b). Cut apart the mini-book pages along the solid lines. Each book will have 8 pages (including the cover).

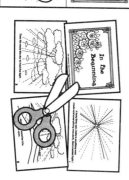

3. Put the pages in order with the cover on top. Staple the pages on the left side to make the book. (Depending on age level, it may be easier to color the illustrations before the books are assembled.)

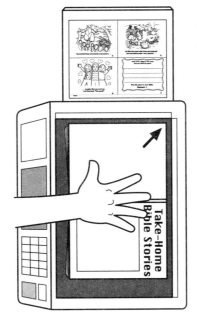

In the Beginning

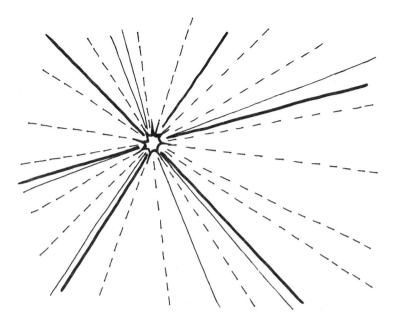

In the beginning, God created the heavens and the earth, and said, "Let there be light."

1

Then, He made the sky to hold the light . . .

2

. . . and the ground for it to shine upon.

3

He planted trees and plants everywhere.

4

He filled the land with birds and animals and something else—very special . . .

5

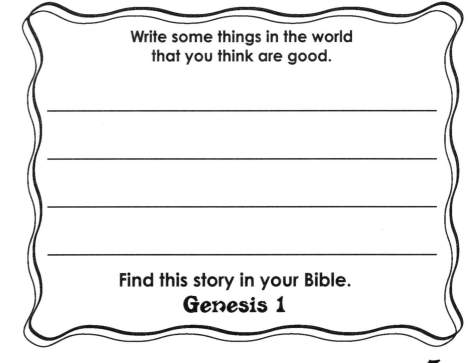

. . . people, like you and me.
And God said, "It is good!"

6

Write some things in the world
that you think are good.

_____

_____

_____

_____

Find this story in your Bible.
Genesis 1

7

Adam and Eve

God wanted to show His glory on earth, so He made a man out of dust and breathed life into him.

1

God called the man Adam.

2

God wanted Adam to have a friend.

3

But there was no one else like Adam.

4

So God took a rib from Adam,
and made a woman named Eve.

5

Together, Adam and Eve cared
for God's beautiful garden.

6

Name some friends that God has given you.

_____

_____

_____

_____

Find this story in your Bible.
Genesis 2:21

7

The First Sin

© Carson-Dellosa CD-0498 Old Testament Take-Home Bible Stories

God loved Adam and Eve.
He gave them a garden to tend.

1

Because the Lord knew what was good for
Adam and Eve, He gave them rules to follow.

2

The devil wanted to cause trouble.
He appeared to Eve in the form of a snake.

3

Satan influenced Adam and Eve to doubt what God had told them. "Did God really say that?" he asked.

4

Adam and Eve took the bait! They ate from the tree God had forbidden. Then, they tried to hide from God.

5

Adam and Eve had to leave the garden because they had made the devil their boss—instead of God.

6

Write some rules that keep you safe.

_____

_____

_____

_____

Find this story in your Bible.

Genesis 3:1

7

Cain
and
Abel

Cain and Abel were brothers.

1

Abel was thankful for the things God gave him.

2

The Lord encouraged Cain to be thankful, too.

3

Cain was jealous of Abel and angry because he thought God loved Abel more. Cain killed Abel.

4

Cain's sin caused him to live under a curse. Life was hard for Cain.

5

Cain had to move far away, but God made a way for him to be protected from his enemies.

6

God loves everyone the same. But everyone doesn't love God the same. How can you show God that you love Him?

_____

_____

_____

Find this story in your Bible.
Genesis 4:1

7

Noah's Ark

Man's sin once became so great that a flood covered the earth. But God protected Noah and his family.

1

The Lord told Noah to build an ark for his family and to fill it with every kind of animal.

2

Water poured from the heavens and sprang up from under the earth.

3

When the ground was dry, Noah and his family and all of the animals left the ark.

4

They thanked God for keeping them safe.

5

God put a rainbow in the sky as His promise that water would never cover the earth again.

6

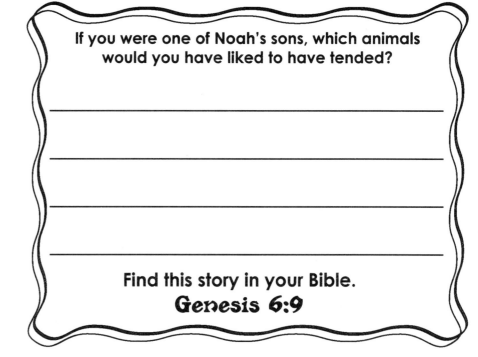

If you were one of Noah's sons, which animals would you have liked to have tended?

_____

_____

_____

_____

Find this story in your Bible.
Genesis 6:9

7

The Tower of Babel

Once there were people who thought they could do anything. They started to build a tower to the sky.

1

But God knew they couldn't make the sun shine, the winds blow, the sky blue, or the grass grow.

2

They couldn't make clouds come, rain fall, streams run, or trees grow.

3

They couldn't make the moon glow, stars fall, night pass, or morning birds call.

4

They couldn't do any of these things.

5

So God gave them different languages to speak. They couldn't finish building the tower.

6

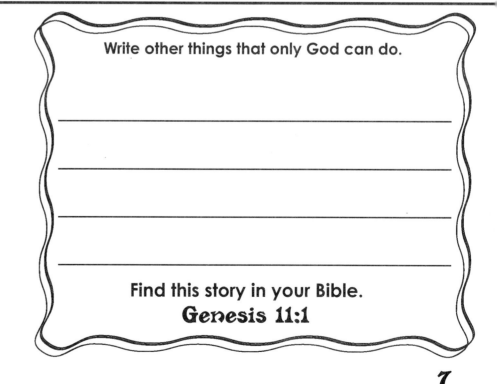

Write other things that only God can do.

_____

_____

_____

_____

_____

Find this story in your Bible.

Genesis 11:1

7

God Sends Abram
to a
New Land

God knew Abram was faithful, so He gave him a special task.

1

He said, "Abram, pack up all your things . . ."

2

". . . bring your family . . ."

3

"... and your animals."

4

Because Abram was faithful, he obeyed.

6

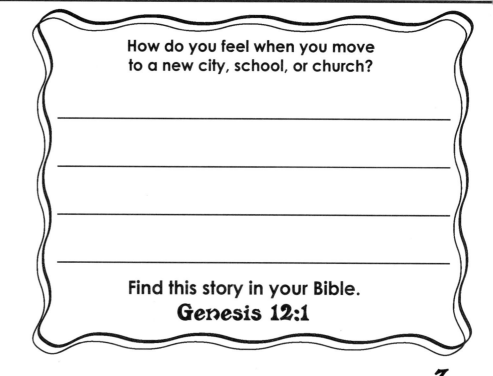

"I'm going to give you a new home far away."

5

How do you feel when you move to a new city, school, or church?

_____

_____

_____

_____

Find this story in your Bible.

Genesis 12:1

7

God's Promise

God told Abram to go for a walk. Abram always obeyed God, so he went into the night.

1

God said, "Don't be afraid. I will protect and reward you."

2

Abram told God that he wanted his own child.

3

God said, "Count the stars." But there were more than Abram could count.

4

God said, "That's how many children and grandchildren I'm going to give you."

5

Abram believed the Lord!

6

God's blessings are always more than we can count. Write as many as you have room for.

_____

_____

_____

_____

Find this story in your Bible.
Genesis 15:1

7

Jacob Wrestles with God

© Carson-Dellosa CD-0498 Old Testament Take-Home Bible Stories

One night Jacob slept under the stars.

1

Suddenly a visitor appeared!

2

He wrestled with Jacob.

3

Page 31

They wrestled with each other until the sun came up.

4

When Jacob began to win, he hurt his leg. The visitor said, "From now on your name is Israel." That meant that Jacob would be the father of a whole nation!

5

After the visitor left, Jacob discovered that he had wrestled with God!

6

How did God show Jacob the plans that He had for his life?

_____

_____

_____

_____

Find this story in your Bible.
Genesis 32:22

7

Jacob's Dream

Jacob was scared and alone.

1

He had made his family mad.

2

He had run away.

3

Now he had no home and just a rock for a pillow.

4

Then, God spoke to him in a dream.

5

"Don't worry, Jacob. Nothing bad will happen to you. And, one day I will even give you all this land."

6

Why does God do good things for us when we are not always good to Him?

_____

_____

_____

_____

Find this story in your Bible.
Genesis 28:10

7

A Brother's Forgiveness

After years away from his family,
Jacob decided it was time to go home.

1

He missed his parents, but thought that
Esau was angry and might try to get even.

2

But God had told him it was time to return.

3

Jacob saw his brother from far away.

4

He wondered what would happen.

5

Esau hugged Jacob and
welcomed him. He was forgiven.

6

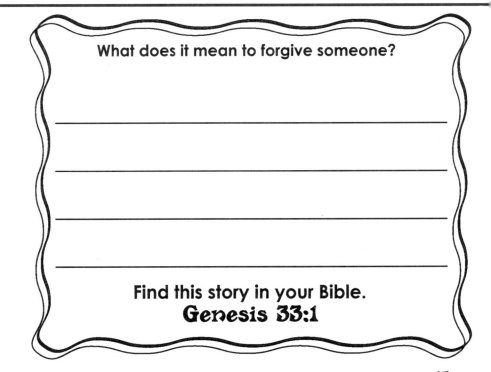

What does it mean to forgive someone?

_____

_____

_____

_____

Find this story in your Bible.
Genesis 33:1

7

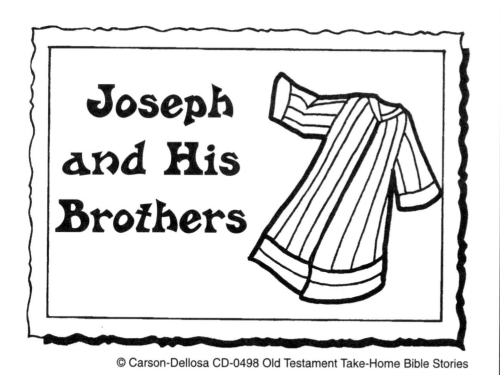

Joseph and His Brothers

Joseph's father gave him a special coat. His brothers were jealous.

1

Joseph had dreams that he was greater than his brothers.

2

This made them hate Joseph. They sold him as a slave.

3

Years later, the brothers came to Egypt where Joseph was a very powerful man.

4

The brothers were afraid that Joseph would be mad.

5

But God had blessed Joseph and caused him to forgive and forget the pain they had caused him.

6

What does it mean to be jealous?
Is it a good or bad thing?

_____

_____

_____

_____

Find this story in your Bible.
Genesis 37:1

7

Slaves in Egypt

Pharaoh was afraid of the Hebrew people.
"What if they try to take over?" he wondered.

1

God's people wanted to live in peace and freedom.

2

Pharaoh made them serve him as slaves. The harder
he worked them, the stronger they became.

3

Page 37

God's people cried for God to help them.

4

God saw their suffering.

5

He had a plan to send a special man named . . .

6

Who do you think God sent to rescue His people from Egypt: Adam, Noah, or Moses?

_____

_____

_____

_____

Find this story in your Bible.
Exodus 1:8

7

Pharaoh was so afraid of God's people, he began killing their boy babies. Then, Moses was born.

1

Moses' parents were not afraid of Pharaoh's orders.

2

His mother prepared a little basket . . .

3

. . . and hid Moses in the Nile River.

4

At the perfect moment, a princess came along . . .

5

. . .and raised him as her son.

6

How did Moses' mother show faith in God?

_____

_____

_____

_____

Find this story in your Bible.
Exodus 2:1

7

The First Passover

Moses warned Pharaoh about the plagues.

1

But Pharaoh always said, "No!"

2

God told Moses to tell His people to put lambs' blood over their doors on a certain night.

All the firstborn of Egypt died that night,
but all who put the blood on their doors were safe.

4

God told His people to continue
to remember and celebrate this day.

5

Jesus celebrated what came to be known as
Passover. Jesus became the Passover lamb.

6

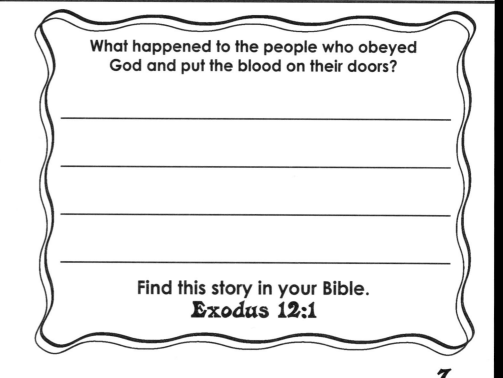

What happened to the people who obeyed
God and put the blood on their doors?

_____

_____

_____

_____

Find this story in your Bible.
Exodus 12:1

7

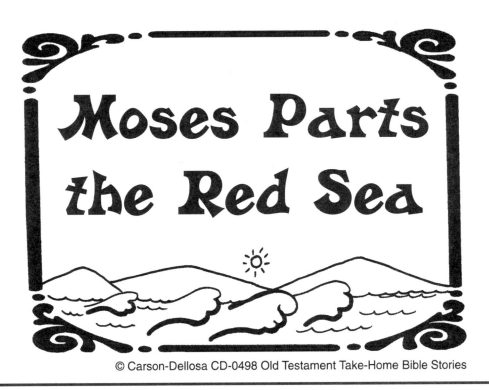

Moses Parts the Red Sea

God's people rejoiced as they left Egypt—
they were no longer slaves!

1

Then, they heard noises! The Egyptian army
was behind them, coming to get them back.

2

They had nowhere to run—
in front of them was the Red Sea.

3

God told Moses to raise his staff and
stretch out his hand over the sea.

4

The sea parted and the Hebrews
walked across on dusty ground.

5

After the Hebrews passed through, God told
Moses to lift his hand again. The waters came back
together and swept the Egyptian army away!

6

What did Moses do to
cause the waters to move?

_____

_____

_____

_____

Find this story in your Bible.
Exodus 13:17

7

God Leads His People in the Desert

God took care of His people in the desert. He delivered them from enemies like Pharaoh's army.

1

The Lord led the way in a cloud by day, and in a fire by night.

2

When they were thirsty, He provided water from a rock.

3

When they were hungry,
He provided bread from the sky . . .

4

. . . and meat for them to eat.

5

God did this because He loved His people
and wanted them to love Him, too.

6

God provided everything the Hebrews needed.
Write some things that God provides for you.

_____

_____

_____

_____

Find this story in your Bible.
Exodus 13:21

7

Friends Help Win a War

As long as Moses held his arms up, God's people were winning a war with people who wanted to hurt them.

1

But wars can last a long time. Moses' arms grew tired and started to drop . . .

2

. . . and God's people started to lose.

3

Then, Aaron and Hur held Moses' arms in the air . . .

4

...and God's people won the war . . .

5

. . . thanks to God . . . and Moses' two friends.

6

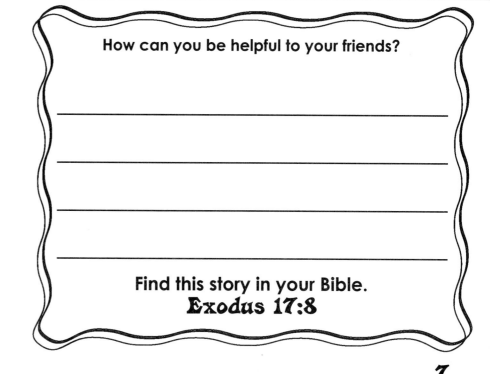

How can you be helpful to your friends?

Find this story in your Bible.
Exodus 17:8

7

Ten Commandments

On Mt. Sinai, God gave rules to Moses to give to His people. He wrote them on stone tablets.

1

Moses carried the tablets back to the people.

2

When Moses got to the camp, he saw that the people had forgotten God.

3

Moses was so angry that he broke the tablets.

4

But the rules were so important
that God wrote them down again.

5

Finally the people learned the Ten Commandments.

6

Why are the Ten Commandments so important?

_____

_____

_____

_____

Find this story in your Bible.
Exodus 31:18

7

The Golden Calf

Moses went up the mountain to talk to God.

1

The Hebrews became nervous.
"Where's Moses? Who will lead us?"

2

They tried to make a god that would lead them.
They melted gold jewelry into the shape of a calf.

3

They worshipped it, but it didn't listen
or talk to them or lead them anywhere.

4

Moses came back and saw what they were doing.

5

Moses said, "There's only one God. He's the
only one you should ever worship."

6

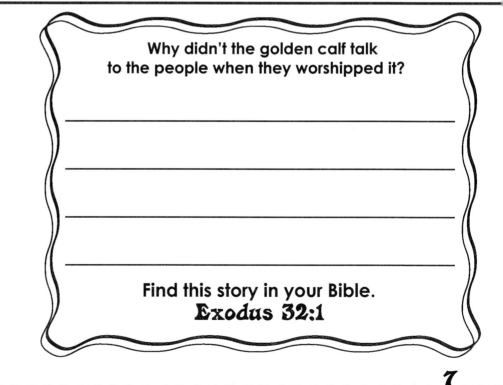

Why didn't the golden calf talk
to the people when they worshipped it?

_____

_____

_____

_____

Find this story in your Bible.
Exodus 32:1

7

A Bright Shining Face

God likes to talk to His people. Even though God loved His people, they were afraid of Him.

1

Moses knew God was loving, and he loved to talk to Him.

2

The people told Moses that they would listen to him, but that they didn't want God to speak to them.

3

The Lord spoke to Moses on Mount Sinai.

4

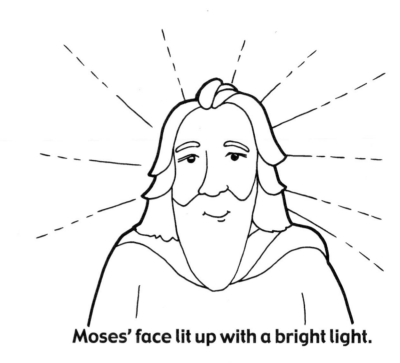

Moses' face lit up with a bright light.

5

When Moses returned to camp, he had to cover his face because it shone from speaking with the Lord.

6

Why did the Hebrew people not want to talk to God?

_____

_____

_____

_____

_____

Find this story in your Bible.
Exodus 34:29

7

The Bronze Snake

While traveling through the desert, some of God's people became sick.

1

They didn't know what to do, so they asked Moses for help.

2

Moses asked God for help.

3

God told Moses to put a bronze snake on a stick, and to hold it up for everyone to see.

4

Everyone who looked at the snake became healthy.

5

God used Moses to heal His people.

6

Who does God use to heal His people today?

_____

_____

_____

_____

_____

Find this story in your Bible.
Numbers 21:8

7

God Chooses a New Leader

Moses led God's people through the desert for 40 years.

1

It was time for someone else to lead God's people.
But where could a leader as good as Moses be found?

2

God had prepared a man to lead His people.

3

That man was Joshua. Joshua had
been a faithful helper to Moses.

4

God had prepared Joshua to lead the people.

5

Joshua led God's people to their new home.

6

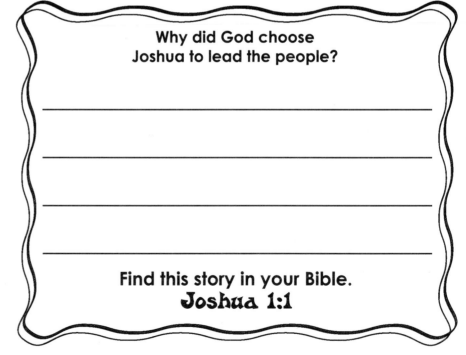

Why did God choose
Joshua to lead the people?

_____

_____

_____

_____

Find this story in your Bible.
Joshua 1:1

7

Bringing Down the Wall of Jericho

Jericho was a city surrounded by a big stone wall.
No one went out, and no one came in.

1

But God told Joshua to lead His people into the city.

2

Joshua led the people around the city seven times.
They were not to speak until he told them to shout.

3

On the seventh day, Joshua commanded the people, "Shout! For the Lord has given you the city!"

4

The priests blew the trumpets and all the people shouted!

5

The wall came tumbling down! God's people entered the city.

6

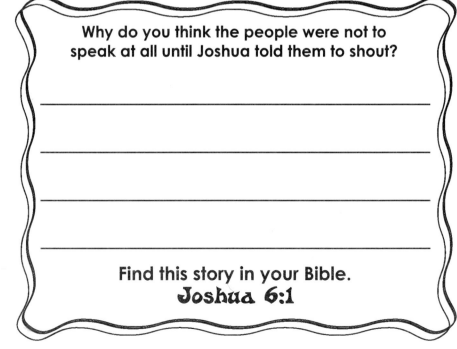

Why do you think the people were not to speak at all until Joshua told them to shout?

_____

_____

_____

_____

Find this story in your Bible.
Joshua 6:1

7

Deborah

Deborah was a leader of God's people

1

She tried to find a man to lead the army . . .

2

. . . but everyone was scared.

3

She picked 10,000 men and led them to war.

4

Everyone was amazed because
the Israelites won the war!

5

Deborah was not amazed. She knew God
had helped her. She sang a song to thank God.

6

Why wasn't Deborah surprised
that the Israelites won the war?

_____

_____

_____

_____

Find this story in your Bible.
Judges 4:1

7

Gideon

An angel of God came with a message for Gideon.
He said God wanted Gideon to lead His people.

1

"There must be some mistake, I am a weak man . . ."

2

". . . and I come from such a small family."

3

But the angel said, "The Lord will be with you!"

4

With God's help, Gideon became a powerful leader.

5

Gideon told people that their real leader was God.

6

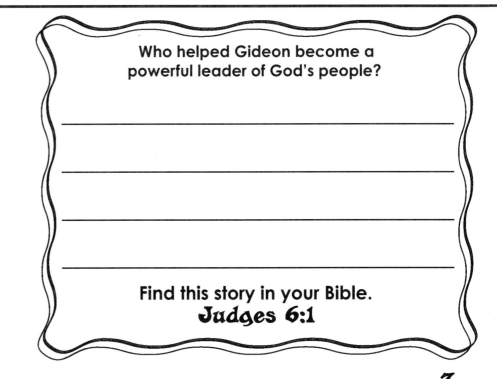

Who helped Gideon become a powerful leader of God's people?

_____

_____

_____

_____

Find this story in your Bible.
Judges 6:1

7

Samson

Samson's mother was so happy to have her baby boy.

1

An angel told her, "He is special. Never cut his hair. He will deliver God's people from the Philistines."

2

She said, "God gave me this baby and I want to obey."

3

Samson grew up to be very strong.

4

He killed a lion with his bare hands.

5

And he served God by fighting the Philistines.

6

Why did Samson's mother obey God?

_____

_____

_____

_____

Find this story in your Bible.
Judges 13:1

7

Samson
Gets His
Strength
Back

God gave Samson strength to protect His people.
When he lost his strength, he became a prisoner.

1

But he had told his secret and lost God's special gift.

2

He prayed to the Lord and asked Him to forgive him.

3

He asked God for strength one more time to get revenge on the Philistines for blinding him.

4

God answered his prayer and Samson became strong again.

5

He pushed hard on two pillars and destroyed the building where his enemies were.

6

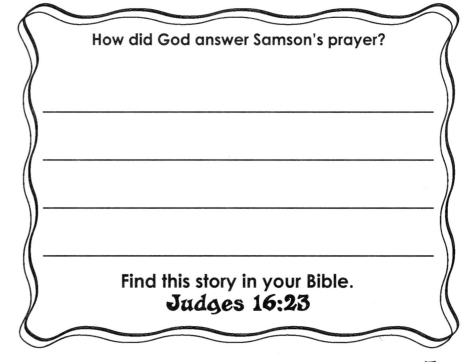

How did God answer Samson's prayer?

_____

_____

_____

_____

Find this story in your Bible.
Judges 16:23

7

Ruth and Naomi

A famine in Judah caused Naomi's family to move to Moab. There, her husband and two sons died.

1

She had two daughters-in-law, Ruth and Orpah.

2

Naomi told them to find husbands and happier lives.

3

Naomi heard that crops were growing again in Judah. She, Ruth, and Orpah decided to move there.

4

Then, Naomi changed her mind.
She told Ruth and Orpah to go back to Moab.
But Ruth refused to leave her.

5

"Naomi, you are my family. I will go wherever you go."

6

Name the people in your family.

_____

_____

_____

_____

_____

Find this story in your Bible.
Ruth 1:1

7

Ruth and Boaz

Ruth and Naomi wondered where they would get food. They were poor and didn't have jobs.

1

Naomi told Ruth to gather leftover grain from a field.

2

A relative of Ruth's, Boaz, owned the field. He saw Ruth and called one of his men aside.

3

"Leave lots of grain for that girl to take home."

4

Ruth thanked Boaz.

5

Boaz married Ruth and cared for her and Naomi.
Ruth, a non-Jewish woman from Moab, became
the great-grandmother of King David!

6

What are some things that Ruth did to show
loyalty to Naomi? How did the Lord bless Ruth?

_____

_____

_____

_____

Find this story in your Bible.
Ruth 2-4

7

A Mother's Sacrifice

Hannah prayed in the temple for a baby.

1

She promised that if she had a son,
he would work in God's temple.

2

A priest heard her and said,
"God will answer your prayer."

3

Soon, Hannah had a baby. She named him Samuel, which means "because I asked God for him."

4

When Samuel was three, Hannah took him to the temple. She asked Eli, the priest, to train Samuel.

5

Hannah said a happy prayer of thanksgiving to God.

6

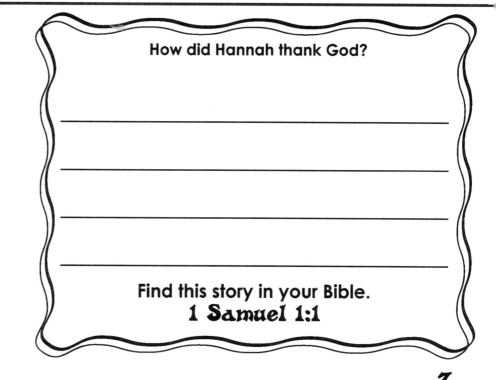

How did Hannah thank God?

_____

_____

_____

_____

Find this story in your Bible.
1 Samuel 1:1

7

God Calls Samuel

Samuel lived at the temple. One night,
a voice woke him, saying "Samuel!"

1

Samuel ran to Eli, "Here I am."

2

But Eli said,
"Go back to bed, I didn't call you."

3

When Samuel lay down, he heard his name again,
"Samuel!" He ran to Eli who sent him to bed—again.

4

Again, Samuel heard his name. Again, he ran to Eli.

5

Now, Eli knew the Lord was calling Samuel. Next time,
Samuel said, "Speak, Lord, your servant is listening."

6

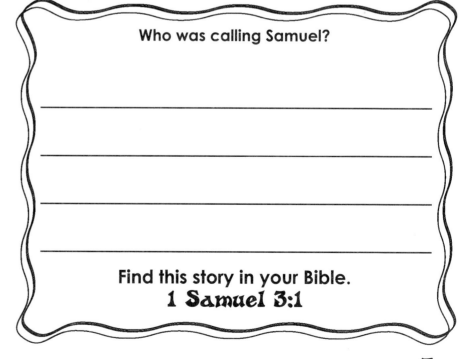

Who was calling Samuel?

_____

_____

_____

_____

Find this story in your Bible.
1 Samuel 3:1

7

A King Loses His Crown

God made Saul king. He wanted to help Saul to lead the people.

1

God helped Saul by telling him what to do.

2

But Saul wouldn't listen. He wanted to do things his way.

3

Saul did things that weren't good for God's people.

4

Samuel told Saul that God was sorry He had made him king.

5

As Samuel left, Saul grabbed his robe. Samuel said, "So has the Lord torn the kingdom away from you!"

6

What happened when Saul disobeyed God?

_____

_____

_____

_____

Find this story in your Bible.
1 Samuel 15:1

7

God's Choice for King

God told Samuel to go to Jesse's house in Bethlehem.
"I have chosen one of his sons to be king."

1

Jesse lined up his sons. They were all big and brave.

2

"Don't you have any other sons?" Samuel asked.

3

Just one. His name is David.
But he is just a boy, not a king.

4

"Just as I suspected . . . this is
the one God sent me to find."

5

Right there, Samuel put oil on David's
head and anointed him king of Israel.

6

Why was David an unusual choice for king?

_____

_____

_____

_____

_____

Find this story in your Bible.
1 Samuel 16:1

7

David and Goliath

Goliath was a giant and an enemy of God's people.

1

Everyday he yelled for an Israelite to fight him.
Even the bravest men were afraid of Goliath.

2

David knew God would be with him and volunteered
to fight Goliath with just his slingshot and stones.

3

When Goliath saw David, he began to laugh.

4

David's stone hit its mark—right between the eyes. Goliath's army ran away.

5

God used a little boy to save the day.

6

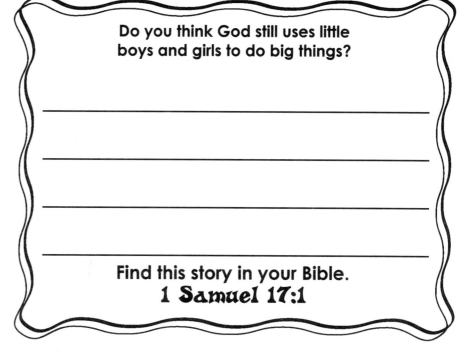

Do you think God still uses little boys and girls to do big things?

_____

_____

_____

_____

Find this story in your Bible.
1 Samuel 17:1

7

Special Friends

Saul was jealous of David. He hated David even though he and his son Jonathan were friends.

1

One day, Saul asked Jonathan to bring David to him. Jonathan knew his father wanted to hurt David.

2

But instead of bringing David to Saul, Jonathan met him in a field and warned him to run away.

3

David and Jonathan hugged because they knew they might not see each other again.

4

When David went away, Jonathan was glad he would be safe.

5

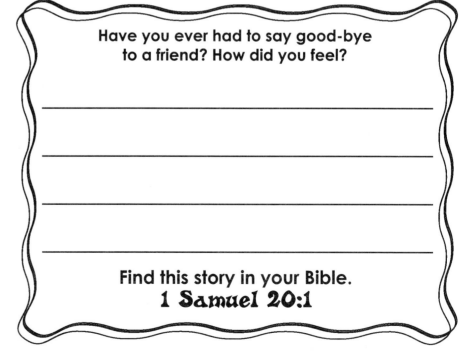

David waved good-bye. He was thankful for a friend like Jonathan.

6

Have you ever had to say good-bye to a friend? How did you feel?

_____

_____

_____

_____

Find this story in your Bible.
1 Samuel 20:1

7

Mercy for Saul

Saul followed David everywhere he went. He wanted to kill David.

1

David trusted the Lord to keep him safe.

2

One day he found Saul standing in a cave. It was a chance to hurt Saul.

3

David knew it would be wrong to
hurt Saul. David walked away.

4

Saul saw David and knew that
David had shown him mercy.

5

Saul was so thankful, he began to cry. He promised
David that he would stop trying to kill him.

6

What is mercy?

_____

_____

_____

_____

Find this story in your Bible.
1 Samuel 24:1

7

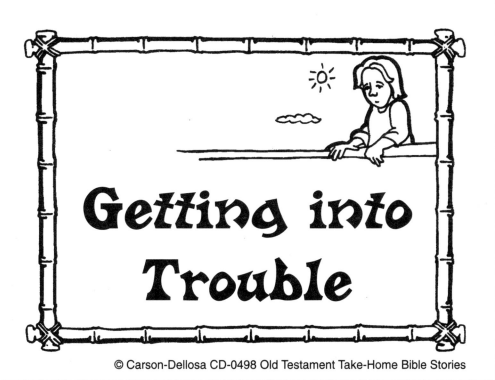

Getting into Trouble

© Carson-Dellosa CD-0498 Old Testament Take-Home Bible Stories

David saw a beautiful woman in the house next to his. Her name was Bathsheba. He wanted to marry her.

1

But Bathsheba was already married to the brave warrior, Uriah.

2

David arranged for Uriah to be killed in battle. Then, David married Bathsheba.

3

The prophet Nathan told David that his actions had displeased the Lord.

4

David admitted that he had sinned and the Lord forgave him.

5

Because David knew what he did was wrong, God let him be king for many more years.

6

Do you ever need to say, "I'm sorry," to God?

_____

_____

_____

_____

Find this story in your Bible.
2 Samuel 11:1

7

Trouble at Home

David's son Absalom had beautiful long hair. He was also a troublemaker who wanted to be king.

1

He tried to convince everyone to make him king instead of his father.

2

He chased his father from the kingdom.

3

When David sneaked back, Absalom fled.

4

As he rode away, Absalom's
hair got caught in a tree and he died.

5

David wept. He loved his son. He cried, "Absalom,
my son, if only I could have died instead of you!"

6

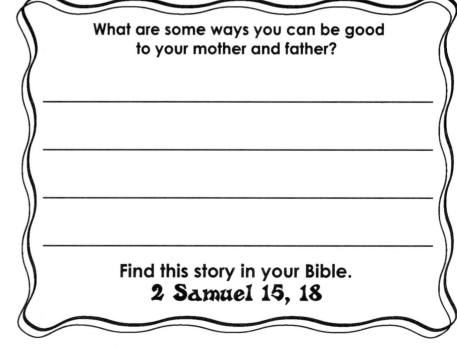

What are some ways you can be good
to your mother and father?

_____

_____

_____

_____

_____

Find this story in your Bible.
2 Samuel 15, 18

7

Singing to God

When David was young, he protected his father's sheep.

1

When David was a man, he was a king who protected God's people.

2

All of his life, David was a musician and a songwriter. He wrote songs praising the goodness of God.

3

**He wrote songs about times
when he needed God's help.**

4

**He wrote songs when he was thankful
for the things God did for him.**

5

**David wrote many songs that we still sing today.
David's songs are part of the book of Psalms.**

6

Make up your own song to sing to God.

_____

_____

_____

_____

Find David's Psalms in your Bible.
Psalms

7

The Best Wish

When David grew old, his son Solomon became king.

1

God granted Solomon one wish. He thought hard.

2

Should he ask for all the money in the world?

3

Should he ask for the biggest palace?

4

Solomon knew he would need God's help to be a good king. Solomon asked God for wisdom.

5

God was pleased with Solomon's request. He made Solomon the wisest man before or since.

6

If God gave you one wish, what would it be?

_____

_____

_____

_____

Find this story in your Bible.

1 Kings 3:1

7

Building a Temple for God

Solomon was a good king who loved God very much.

1

Solomon said, "I have a nice house. God should have an even nicer temple."

2

Solomon spent seven years building the temple.

3

The ark of the Covenant was placed in the temple. It held the stone tablets that Moses had placed in it.

4

God told Solomon that as long as the people obeyed the commandments He would be among them.

5

Never before was there such a beautiful temple.

6

Where is the temple that
God wants to dwell in today?

_____

_____

_____

_____

Find this story in your Bible.
1 Kings 6:1

7

Fed
by
Ravens

The Lord sent His prophet Elijah
to give King Ahab bad news.

1

Elijah said, "There will be no rain for a long time."
That meant food and water would be hard to find.

2

This news made King Ahab angry. The Lord
told Elijah about a secret place to live.

3

There, Elijah found a stream to drink from.

4

God sent ravens to Elijah every morning and evening with bread and meat.

5

Elijah was thankful that God provided for him.

6

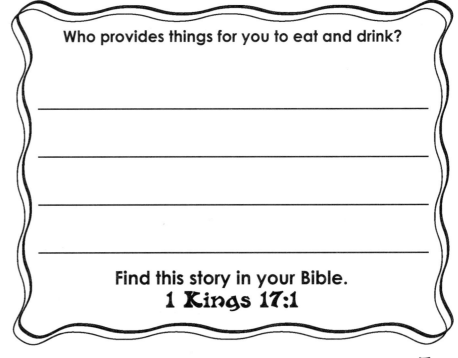

Who provides things for you to eat and drink?

_____

_____

_____

_____

Find this story in your Bible.
1 Kings 17:1

7

Elijah and the Widow

When Elijah was traveling, he became hungry and thirsty. God told him to visit a widowed woman.

1

The woman told Elijah that she was running out of flour and oil for herself and her son.

2

Because Elijah knew God would provide, he told the woman to cook a meal for him from the flour and oil.

3

Every time they ate, they found more flour
and oil in the jars. They had plenty of food.

4

One day the woman's son died. She told Elijah.
He asked God to bring life back to the boy and He did.

5

God provided for Elijah and the woman who helped him.

6

What can you share with the people
who teach you about the Lord?

_____

_____

_____

_____

_____

Find this story in your Bible.
1 Kings 17:7

7

God's New Prophet

Everywhere the prophet Elijah went, Elisha followed.

1

Time and again, Elijah told him to stay, but Elisha would say, "As sure as God lives, I will not leave you."

2

Elijah's time as a prophet was coming to an end. He said to Elisha, "What is it you want from me?"

3

Elisha said, "I want to be a prophet like you—only twice as good!"

4

Elijah said, "That's quite a wish. But if you see me as I am taken into heaven, it will happen!"

5

Elisha saw a chariot of fire take Elijah into heaven. Elisha became God's new prophet.

6

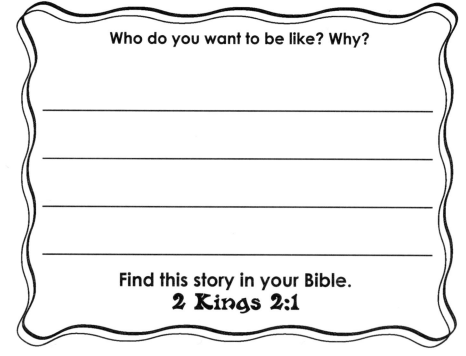

Who do you want to be like? Why?

_____

_____

_____

_____

Find this story in your Bible.
2 Kings 2:1

7

Obeying God's Word

Josiah was king in Jerusalem. He noticed that God's temple needed to be repaired.

1

The temple workers found a book of the law that God had made for His people. They took it to Josiah.

2

Josiah was shocked! The people had forgotten these laws. Josiah apologized to God.

3

He gathered all the people and read the book to them.

4

He told them they must all begin to obey the laws.

5

All of Jerusalem began to praise the Lord!

6

Where do you hear God's Word being read?

_____

_____

_____

_____

_____

Find this story in your Bible.
2 Kings 22:1

7

Northern and Southern Kingdoms

© Carson-Dellosa CD-0498 Old Testament Take-Home Bible Stories

God's people began to forget all the good things the Lord had done for them.

1

They stopped worshipping Him and even started worshipping gods that don't exist.

2

They did terrible things to each other because they forgot to live by God's rules.

3

The Babylonians came to Jerusalem and broke down the walls and burned the city.

4

They took God's people away and made them serve their king.

5

The Lord waited patiently for His people's hearts to change and for them to begin to call on Him again.

6

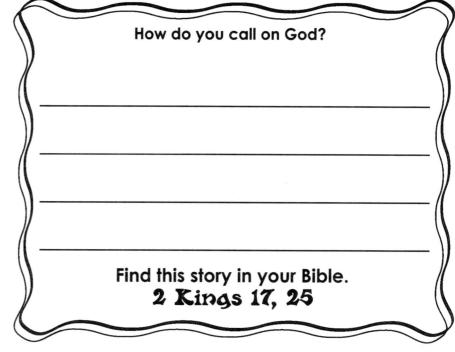

How do you call on God?

_____

_____

_____

_____

_____

Find this story in your Bible.
2 Kings 17, 25

7

Rebuilding the Temple

God's people were sorry for forgetting God.
They called on Him to bring them home.

1

Their houses had been taken from them.

2

God's people wandered until they came to Persia.

3

The Persian king heard about the temple and told God's people to return home and rebuild it.

4

Men worked many days to rebuild the temple.

5

God's people gathered to celebrate and to praise God.

6

What are some ways you can make your church a nicer place?

_____

_____

_____

_____

_____

Find this story in your Bible.
Ezra 1, 6

7

Taking a Stand for God

Mordecai was a good man who knew that he should worship only God.

1

The Persian king made a law that everyone should bow to Haman, one of his officials.

2

But Mordecai would not bow. Haman was shocked and very angry. He plotted to hurt Mordecai.

3

Page 113

Haman went to the king to
ask that Mordecai be hanged.

4

Before Haman could speak, the king said he wanted to
honor Mordecai. He had just found out that Mordecai had
saved his life and had never been rewarded for it.

5

The king made Haman lead Mordecai
around the city on the king's own horse.

6

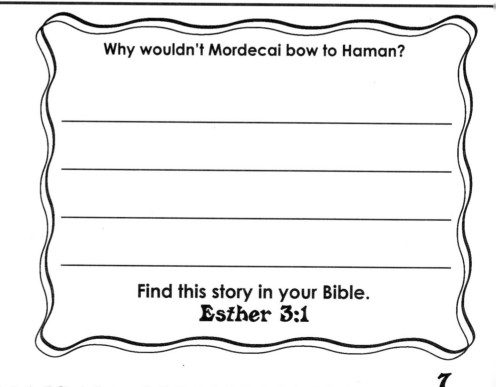

Why wouldn't Mordecai bow to Haman?

_____

_____

_____

_____

_____

Find this story in your Bible.
Esther 3:1

7

Brave Queen Esther

Haman and the king planned to kill the Jewish people.
Mordecai told his cousin, Queen Esther, about the plot.

1

The king didn't know that Esther was Jewish.
If she asked him for help, he might kill her.

2

But Esther wanted to help her people.
She prayed about what to do.

3

Esther fasted and prayed and then told the king about the plot to kill the Jews.

4

The king admired Esther's bravery and stopped the plot against the Jewish people.

5

God used Queen Esther to save many lives.

6

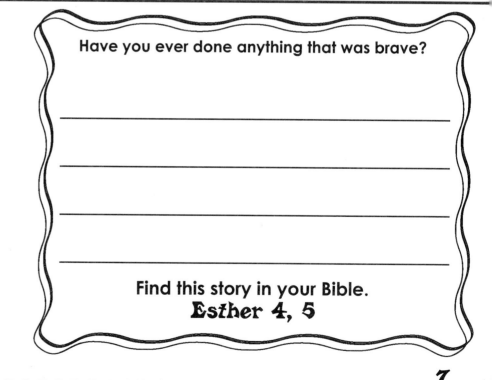

Have you ever done anything that was brave?

_____

_____

_____

_____

Find this story in your Bible.
Esther 4, 5

7

Job

Job was a good man who loved God very much.

1

Satan told God that he could cause Job to hate God.

2

Satan stole Job's children and riches. Job loved God even though he thought He was taking things away.

3

Satan caused Job to become ill. He still loved God.

4

Job said he didn't know why bad things happened to him but that he loved and trusted God.

5

The Lord gave Job back twice as much as Satan had taken from him.

6

Who gave you the things that you have?

Find this story in your Bible.
Job 1, 42

7

Speaking without Words

Ezekiel was a prophet. The Lord asked him to deliver some messages to His people without using words.

1

The Lord had Ezekiel draw a picture of the city and lay next to it on his side for 390 days. That's over a year!

2

Then, Ezekiel was told to flip over to his other side for another 40 days.

3

Then, God had him cut off his beard and shave his head.

4

God wanted people to stop and notice Ezekiel's strange behavior.

5

Some people figured out what it meant. They had been bad and would be sent away for a long time.

6

What are some ways you could tell someone something without words?

_____

_____

_____

_____

Find this story in your Bible.
Ezekiel 4-5

7

Fiery Furnace

Shadrach, Meshach, and Abednego lived in Babylon and worshipped the true God.

1

King Nebuchadnezzar built a golden statue and commanded that people fall down and worship it.

2

Shadrach, Meshach, and Abednego refused. They would only worship God.

3

The king was furious! "I'll throw you into a furnace and what god will save you?" "Our God will!" they replied.

4

The king made the furnace hotter than ever before and commanded that God's men be thrown in.

5

The king saw an angel in the furnace. He had the men freed and decided to worship the true God.

6

How did God protect Shadrach, Meshach, and Abednego?

_____

_____

_____

_____

_____

Find this story in your Bible.
Daniel 3:1

7

Handwriting on the Wall

King Belshazzar didn't worship God.
He didn't even think about Him.

1

At a party, he bragged about his gold and silver, and served wine in goblets stolen from the temple in Jerusalem.

2

Suddenly, a hand appeared and wrote on the wall.
The king was so frightened that he couldn't stand.

3

The king's wise men were called in to explain what the words meant, but they could not.

4

The king called for Daniel who read the words and said, "It means the party's over and so is your kingdom!"

5

Daniel was made a ruler and later that night, the king died.

6

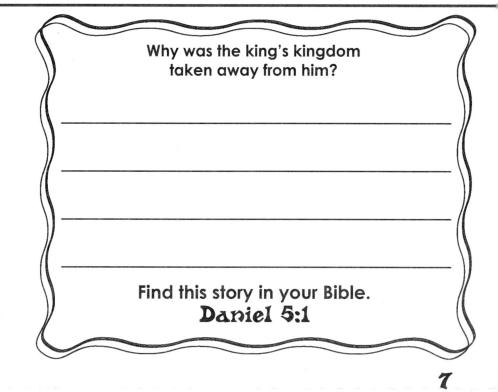

Why was the king's kingdom taken away from him?

_____

_____

_____

_____

Find this story in your Bible.
Daniel 5:1

7

Daniel in the Lions' Den

Daniel prayed to God three times every day.

1

In Babylon, people were only supposed to pray to King Darius.

2

Some people caught Daniel praying to God and brought him to the king.

3

As punishment, Daniel was thrown into a den of lions.

4

But after spending a whole night in the lions' den, Daniel was still alive.

5

The king set Daniel free.

6

How many times a day do you talk with God?

_____

_____

_____

_____

_____

Find this story in your Bible.
Daniel 6:1

7